Chef Skylar's Allergy Cookbook

Eggs, Dairy, and Peanuts

Written by: Skylar McBride
With: Heddrick McBride
Recipes by: Chef Skylar McBride and Chef Cassandra Richardson
Illustrated by: HH-Pax

Dedication

This book is dedicated to everyone with food allergies. As a kid growing up with different allergies, I know how it feels to miss out on good foods because of restrictions. I have searched to find ingredients that will serve as a substitute for common allergy foods without losing the great taste. I hope you enjoy the book and of course the food.

I want to thank all of the people who have helped me on my cooking journey. First, I want to thank my parents for always supporting me. I thank my mom for always helping me experiment with new recipes and my dad for being my personal dishwasher. My Grandmother Paulette has taught me how to make many homemade meals. My Grandfather taught me how to make homemade sauce and corn bread. My Uncle Grallian has taught me how to cook a new dish everytime we visit his house.

My biggest thank you goes to my aunts, Vanessa, Dennett, and Cassandra. My Auntie Vanessa believed in my dream since I was a baby. She has bought most of my cooking supplies and cookbooks. My Auntie Dennett paid for me to attend Young Chef's Academy, where I learned how to improve my cooking skills. She has also sent me Chef Coats and recipes from all over the world. My Auntie Cassandra is the one who I get to practice cooking with. She is a chef, and she has taught me many recipes and cooking techniques. Thank you all for playing such a big part in my young cooking career. I love you all! I also want to give a shout out to all of my friends and teachers at P.S 117. Thank you for enjoying the dishes that I bring to the school.

BREAKFAST RECIPES

Eggless Waffles Recipe

Ingredients

- 2 cups flour
- 4 tsp baking powder
- 2 tsp sugar
- 2 cups milk
- 2 tbsp vegetable oil
- 2 tbsp water
- 1 tsp vanilla
- ½ cup applesauce
- 4 tbsp melted butter
- 1 granny smith apple (peeled, cored and sliced) may use
- canned if available (toss in 1 tbsp. lemon juice and 1 tsp sugar)
- caramel sauce

Directions

- Turn on waffle maker.

- Combine the flour, baking powder and sugar.

- In a separate bowl, mix together milk, oil, water, applesauce, vanilla, and butter.

- Add the wet ingredients to the dry ingredients, and mix together slowly (mix should be slightly lumpy).

- Let stand for 5 minutes (will puff up).

- Once the waffle maker is hot, scoop the butter in (follow the manufacturer's instructions).

- Top with sliced apples and caramel sauce (may add non-dairy topping).

Cereal Substitute

Ingredients

- coco puffs
  *substitute your favorite cereal

- soy silk milk
  *may substitute any dairy
  free or lactose free milk

FOLLOW SERVING SIZE PER YOUR RECOMMENDED DAILY ALLOWANCE.

Peanut Free Granola Recipe

Ingredients

- 4 ½ cups rolled oats (Quaker oats)
- 1 cup flour
- ⅓ cup brown sugar
- ½ cup applesauce
- 2 cups chocolate chips
- 1 cup sunflower seeds
- 1 tsp baking soda
- 1 tsp vanilla extract
- ½ cup honey
- ⅔ cup butter

Mix-ins

- ½ cup coconut flakes
- ⅔ cups craisins (dried cranberries)
- 1 9 x 13 cookie sheet
- 1 microwave safe bowl

Directions

- Preheat oven to 350⁰ F.

- In a large bowl, combine rolled oats, flour, brown sugar, chocolate chips, and baking soda. Mix well.

- Add vanilla, honey, apple sauce, melted butter, and sunflower seeds (you may add other mix-ins).

- Mix and pour in 9 x 13 pan.
  Using a spatula, spread and flatten granola.

- Bake in the oven for 20-30 minutes.

- Remove from the oven and let it cool down for 20 minutes.

Ingredients

Mix-ins

GRANOLA BARS DONE!

LUNCH RECIPES

Eggless Chicken Nuggets

Ingredients

- 1 package skinless chicken tenders
- 1 cup Italian bread crumbs
- ½ cup grated parmesan cheese
- 1 tsp salt

- 1 tsp dried thyme
- 1 tbsp dried basil
- ½ cup butter melted

Directions

- Preheat oven 350° F.

- Cut chicken tenders into 4 pieces.

- In a medium bowl, mix together bread crumbs, cheese, salt, thyme, and basil.

- Melt butter in microwaveable bowl (for dipping).

- Dip chicken into melted butter, then coat with breadcrumbs.

- Place the coated chicken pieces on a greased cookie sheet. Bake for 10 minutes.

STEP 1

STEP 2

NUGGETS READY

Vegetarian Pizza

Ingredients

- flour tortilla
- tofurkey
- spinach

- vegan cheese
- tomato sauce

Directions

- Preheat oven to 350^0F.

- Cube or slice tofurkey.

- Wash spinach leaves.

- Prepare tomato sauce.

- On a cookie tray, lay out the tortilla shell. Sprinkle with vegan cheese. Bake for 10 minutes.

- Spread 4 oz sauce on the tortilla.

- Top with spinach leaves and tofurkey.

- Sprinkle with vegan cheese. Bake for 10 minutes.

Vegetarian Pizza -
Tofurkey, Spinach And Vegan Cheese

Sunflower Butter and Jelly Sandwiches

Ingredients

- 1 jar sunflower butter
- 1 jar grape or strawberry jelly or jam
- 2 slices of honey wheat bread
- toaster

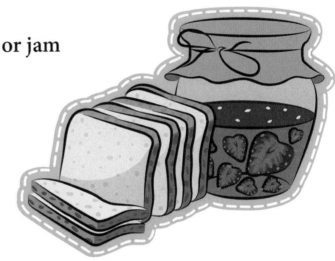

Directions

- Toast 2 slices of honey wheat bread.

- Spread sunflower butter (may use safflower butter, no butter, or check your local grocer for peanut butter substitute).

- Add your favorite jelly/jam.

- Cut into triangles.

Sunflower Butter and Jelly Sandwiches

DINNER RECIPES

Eggless Meatballs

Ingredients

- 1 pound ground beef
- 2 tbsp minced garlic
- 2 tsp dried basil
- 1 tsp salt
- ½ tsp crushed red pepper flakes
- 2 tbsp Worcestershire sauce
- ½ cup milk
- ½ parmesan cheese
- ¾ cups bread crumbs

Directions

- Preheat oven to 350° F.

- In a medium bowl, combine all ingredients.

- Mix until all ingredients have been incorporated.

- Lightly spray pan or baking sheet with pan spray.

- Shape into 1 -2 oz. balls.

- Bake for 20-25 minutes.

Toss in BBQ Sauce
for a Quick Snack!

Serve with
pasta and
alfredo sauce!

Pasta with Coconut Milk Alfredo Sauce

Ingredients

- 1 cup coconut milk
- ¼ tsp dried basil
- 1 tsp salt
- 2 tbsp cornstarch
- 1 tbsp minced garlic
- 1 tsp cooking oil

Directions

- Combine the first 4 ingredients together in a bowl.

- Heat a sauté pan on medium flame.

- Add 1 tbsp. cooking oil and minced garlic.

- Sauté until golden brown.

- Add ingredients in bowl.

- Cook until it reaches the desired consistency.

- Add pasta and serve.

PASTA W/ COCONUT MILK ALFREDO SAUCE

Thai Noodle Salad with Thai Sauce

Ingredients

- mix 4 cups of cabbage, carrots, and radish (shredded or grated)
- 3 scallions, sliced
- ½ bunch cilantro, chopped (or sub basil and mint)
- 1 tablespoon (or less, or more) jalapeño, finely chopped

Thai Sauce

- 3 slices ginger
- 1 fat clove garlic
- ¼ cup butter, sunflower butter
- 1 orange (¼ cup orange juice)
- 1 med-large lime (3 tablespoon lime juice)
- 2 tablespoons soy sauce or GF Braggs Liquid Amino Acids (Note: Tamari will turn this unpleasantly dark)
- 3 tablespoons honey or agave
- 3 tablespoons toasted sesame oil
- ½ -1 teaspoon cayenne pepper (or a squirt of sriracha sauce)
- ½ teaspoon salt
- Sesame Ginger Tofu (Optional) Go to Link

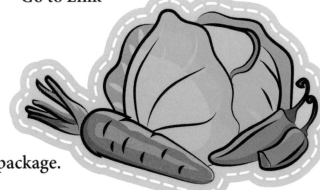

Directions

- Cook pasta according to directions on package.

- Drain and chill under cold water.

- In the meantime, blend the sauce ingredients together in a blender until smooth.

- Place shredded veggies, bell pepper, scallions, cilantro and jalapeño in a bowl.

- Toss.

- Add the cold noodles to the bowl and toss again.

- Pour the sauce over top and toss well to combine.

- Taste, adjust the salt and serve, cilantro and a lime wedge.

Teriyaki Noodle Bowls

Ingredients

TERIYAKI SAUCE:

- ¼ cup soy sauce
- 2 tbsp rice vinegar
- 2 tbsp brown sugar
- ¼ tsp toasted sesame oil
- 2 cloves garlic, minced
- 2 inches fresh ginger, grated
- pinch red pepper flakes, optional
- 1 tbsp cornstarch
- 2 tbsp water

NOODLES & VEGETABLES:

- 1 lb. fresh or frozen stir fry vegetables
- 8 oz. Thai noodles
- 1 tbsp vegetable oil

Directions

- Put the soy sauce, rice vinegar, brown sugar, toasted sesame oil, red pepper flakes, corn starch, and water into a bowl.

- Peel the ginger and then grate it straight into the bowl using a small holed cheese grater. (If you don't have a grater, you can mince the ginger).

- Mince the garlic and add it to the bowl. Stir to combine the ingredients.

- Bring a medium pot of water up to a boil over high heat, add the noodles, and then turn off the flame and let the noodles sit for 5-6 minutes, or until the noodles are tender.

- Drain the noodles in a colander.

- Heat the vegetable oil in a large skillet over medium-high heat.

- Once hot, add the vegetables.

- Stir and cook for only about 3-4 minutes.

- Add the teriyaki sauce and allow it to come up to a simmer, at which point it will thicken. The vegetables will finish heating through as this happens.

- Turn the heat off once the sauce is hot and thick.

- Add the drained noodles to the skillet and stir until they are coated in the sauce.

- Divide the noodles between four bowls and then spoon any leftover vegetables from the skillet on top.

Noodles and Vegetables

ENJOY!

DESSERT RECIPES

Eggless Chocolate Chip Cookies

Ingredients

- ½ cup butter (1 stick) softened
- ¼ cup sugar
- ½ cup packed brown sugar
- 1 ½ cup flour
- 1 tsp baking soda
- 1 tsp vanilla
- 3 tbsp water
- 4 tbsp vegetable oil
- 1 cup chocolate chips

Directions

- Preheat oven to 350° F.

- Beat the butter and sugar(s) together until creamy.

- Add flour and baking soda.

- Add water, oil and vanilla.

- Add chocolate chips.

- Drop spoonfuls of dough onto baking sheets (use two tablespoons) bake for 8-10 minutes or until golden brown.

COOL !

Banana Ice Cream

Ingredients

- 2 cans (13.5 oz. ea.) full fat coconut milk
- ½ can lactose free milk

- 2 tsp vanilla extract
- 2 ripe bananas (mashed)

Directions

- Chill 2 cans of coconut milk in the refrigerator (can be done overnight).

- Open both cans (do not shake – skim / remove the cream from the top).

- Place the cream into a mixing bowl (save the coconut water for a smoothie or for a refreshing drink).

- With an electric beater whip the coconut cream on high until it becomes light and fluffy (like whipped cream).

- Add the lactose free milk and whip on high speed for 2-3 minutes or until mixture thickens.

- Stir in vanilla (optional).

- Add mashed bananas and mix together.

- Transfer to a lidded container and freeze.

Muddy Buddies

Ingredients

- 9 cups Rice Chex(R), Corn Chex(R) (available in other flavors)
- 1 cup semisweet chocolate chips (white chocolate chip substitute)
- ½ cup (no butter, or sunflower butter)

- ¼ cup butter or margarine
- 1 teaspoon vanilla
- 1 ½ cups powdered sugar

Directions

- Measure cereal in a large bowl and set aside.

- In 1-quart microwaveable bowl, microwave chocolate chips and butter uncovered on High 1 minute; stir.

- Microwave about 30 seconds longer or until the mixture can be stirred smoothly.

- Stir in vanilla.

- Pour mixture over cereal, stirring until evenly coated.

- Pour into 2-gallon resealable food-storage plastic bag.

- Add powdered sugar. Seal bag; shake until well coated.

- Spread on waxed paper to cool.

- Refrigerate in an airtight container.

Chef Skylar Bio

Chef Skylar McBride is ten years old and is currently in the 5th grade. She has been cooking since the age of three. Skylar attended Young Chef's Academy Cooking School, where she received all six achievement badges. She completed the course and was awarded the Junior Master Chef's Coat. At the age of eight, Skylar was the youngest contestant of the Master Chef Junior New York City Talent Search. She impressed the judges so much, that she advanced to the final round of auditions. Skylar enjoys cooking for family, friends, and her classmates. Skylar's favorite dish is pasta and scallops. Skylar lives in Queens, New York with her mother Danielle, and her father Heddrick.

CASSANDRA RICHARDSON, CEC, MFP, FMP
ANNE ARUNDEL COMMUNITY COLLEGE

Chef Richardson has obtained distinction as:

- American Culinary Federation (ACF) Certified
- Executive Chef
- MFP – Manage First Professional
- FMP – Foodservice Management Professional
- ServSafe Instructor / Proctor
  — ServSafe Allergens
  — ServSafe Food Handlers
- ServSafe Alcohol Instructor / Proctor
- Manage First Instructor / Proctor
  — Hospitality and Restaurant Management
  — Nutrition

Chef Cassandra Richardson Bio

Chef Cassandra Richardson, CEC has been a Chef /Instructor at Anne Arundel Community College since 2002. She also operates her business, Cassie Cuisine.

Chef Richardson has a passion for teaching, cooking and creativity and shows her love through mentoring and touching the lives of young culinarians. "Being an instructor allows me to share my knowledge, challenge the students' creativity, and provide instruction that will allow them to obtain professional credentials as well as college credits."

Chef Richardson and her students have prepared cuisine for First Lady of The United States Michelle Obama, Secretary of Labor Hon. Hilda Solis, Hon. Elaine Cho, Members of Congress, and World Dignitaries during the G20 Summit. They also had the opportunity to work side by side with Chef Robert Irvine star of the Food Networks "Dinner Impossible" and Chef Ming Tsai star of "East Meets West, Ming's Quest and Simply Ming."

VISIT
WWW.MCBRIDESTORIES.COM
FOR MORE TITLES

Made in the USA
Columbia, SC
19 December 2020